God Dreamed of Me

Written by Melanie Higginbotham
Illustrated by Alessia Lingesso

WestBow Press books may be ordered through booksellers or by contacting:

WestBow Press
A Division of Thomas Nelson & Zondervan
1663 Liberty Drive
Bloomington, IN 47403
www.westbowpress.com
844-714-3454

Interior Image Credit: Alessia Lingesso

ISBN: 978-1-6642-8032-8 (sc)
ISBN: 978-1-6642-8034-2 (hc)
ISBN: 978-1-6642-8033-5 (e)

Library of Congress Control Number: 2022918657

Print information available on the last page.

WestBow Press rev. date: 10/07/2022

WESTBOW
PRESS®
A DIVISION OF THOMAS NELSON
& ZONDERVAN

Author:

Melanie Higginbotham is a wife, mother of three, and a lover of all things that bring joy, especially children. She has lived in several countries and found one thing remained the same: the wide eyed wonder of a child.

She lives in Jacksonville, Florida with her family.

Illustrator:

Alessia Lingesso was born in Taranto (Puglia, south of Italy) 45 years ago and has cultivated her two great passions: animals and illustration. She has been working as a freelance writer for some years and mainly illustrates children's books.

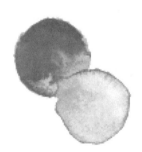

I am God's Dream!
He wanted me to be!
Before I was born
He planted the Seed.

My mommy and daddy
Knew full well
That He was the One
Who created each cell.

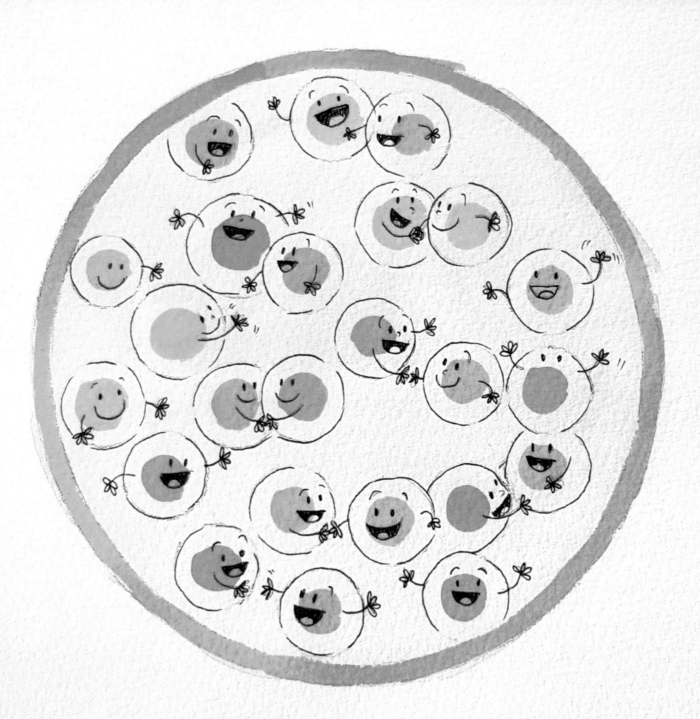

When it was decided
That I would be
A spark was lit and
God set me free!

7

To grow into
The child that He loves
Within my mommy's belly
But born from above.

He chose my skin
My hair and my smile
And grew me in
The most delicate style.

So inward I grew
Nine months to be exact
My heart beating wildly
With nothing to lack.

From her life to mine
I grew through and through
Until heaven was ready
For her to "Dar a Luz."

And with a shout and a bang
I burst forth into light
And gave my first cry
With anticipation and fright.

But she held me close
And whispered to me
"You were God's dream
That He gave to me.

You have a gift
From God above
That isn't the same as mine
And so full of love.

Grow it with grace
And let it be
Because the world needs
You to be free!"

What God sees
When He looks at me
Is pure delight
But, also, mystery.

A gift for His Son
The Beloved One
Who loved me before
The world had begun.

Printed in the United States
by Baker & Taylor Publisher Services